BOBBY HULL
HOCKEY'S GOLDEN JET

BOBBY HULL
HOCKEY'S GOLDEN JET

by Julian May

Published by Crestwood House, Inc., Mankato, Minnesota 56001. Published simultaneously in Canada by J.M. Dent and Sons, Ltd. Library of Congress Catalog Card Number: 74-82741. International Standard Book Number: 0-913940-06-2. Text copyright © 1974 by Julian May Dikty. Illustrations copyright © 1974 by Crestwood House, Inc. All rights reserved. No part of this book may be reproduced in any form without permission from the publisher, except for brief passages included in a review. Printed in the United States of America.

Designed by William Dichtl

PHOTOGRAPHIC CREDITS
Chicago Blackhawks: 17, 35; Publication Associates: 8-9, 11, 12, 13; Michael Semak, from Information Canada Phototique: 10; United Press International: 2, 19, 20, 21, 22, 23, 25, 26, 29, 31, 32, 33, 36, 37, 38, 40, 42, 43, 44; Wide World Photos: 6, 18, 24, 27, 28, 30, 34, 39, 41, 45, 46, 47; Woodstock Ont. Daily Sentinel-Review: 14.
Cover: United Press International.

BOBBY HULL
HOCKEY'S GOLDEN JET

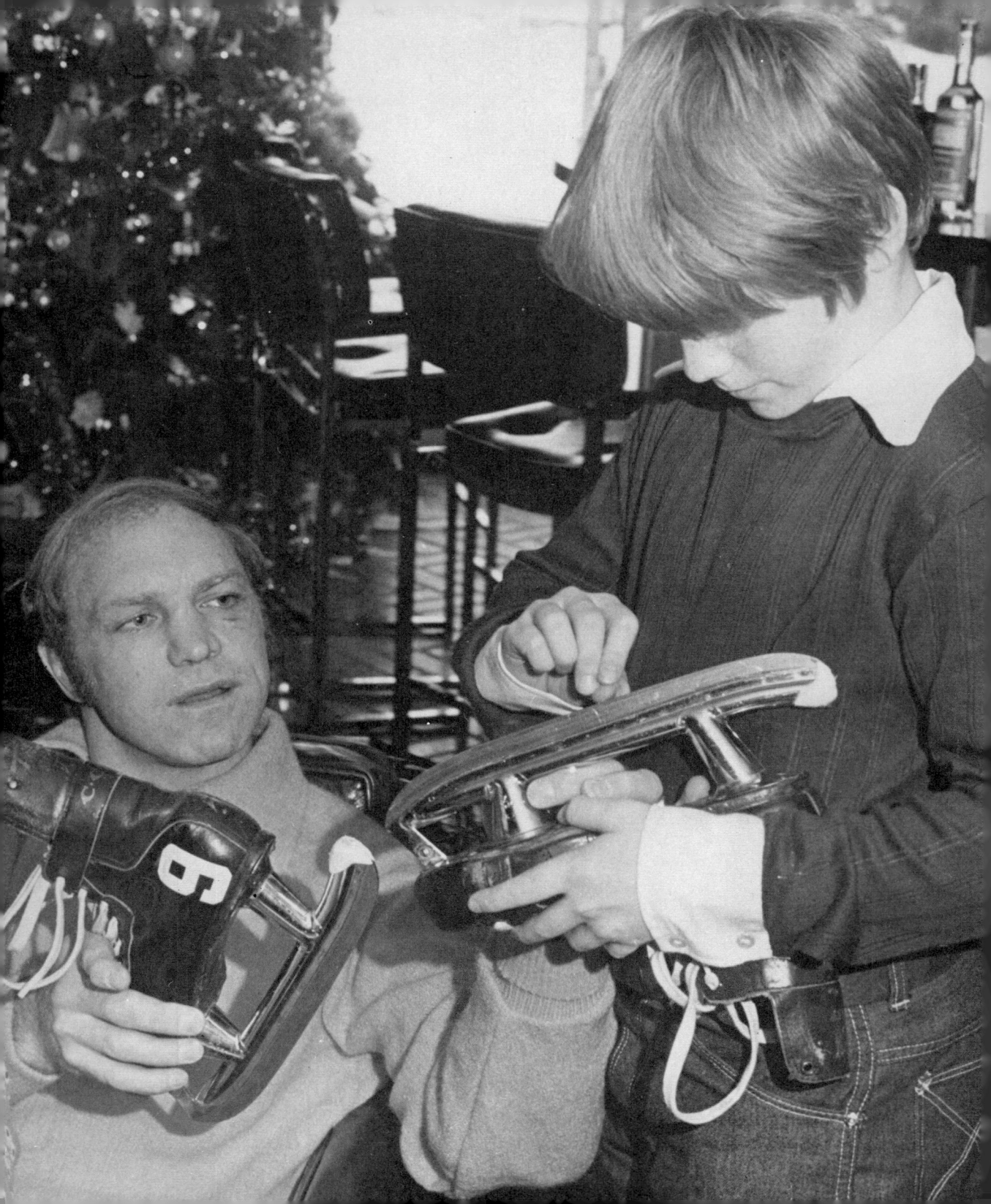

Ice skates for Christmas!

Three-year-old Bobby Hull gave a howl of joy. "I want to skate now!" he said.

His sisters, Jack and Mac, aged six and seven, had received new skates, too. "We'll teach you, Robert," Jack said. "But if you cry when you fall down, back inside you go. We don't want to bother with babies."

"I won't cry," Bobby promised.

Mr. and Mrs. Hull laughed as they watched their three children skate. The "rink" was a patch of ice on the street in front of the General Store. Bobby fell down, but he never cried. His wobbly ankles stiffened up, and within 15 minutes he was skating fairly well.

He loved it. He skated and skated until the sun went down and it began to get dark. His mother called:

"Come inside, Robert! Christmas dinner is ready!"

But he wouldn't stop skating. The only way they could get little Bobby off the ice was to go out and lead him in by the hand.

Perhaps Bobby Hull remembers a long-ago Christmas gift of skates as he celebrates the holiday with his oldest son, Bobby, Jr., in 1973.

This little inlet of the Bay of Quinte was the outdoor hockey rink for the Hull children. In the background are buildings of the cement company where Bobby's father worked as a foreman.

The Hull family lived in Point Anne, Ontario. It was a drab company town built for the workers in a big cement factory. An arm of Lake Ontario—the Bay of Quinte—was only a few hundred yards from the Hull home. Bobby spent many hours skating on the bay ice. He was a natural athlete, born with strong muscles and quick reflexes.

The winters are long and cold in Point Anne. In most years, the kids could play hockey from October to March. Little Bobby spent all his spare time on the ice. Sometimes he even got up before dawn so that he could have the town hockey rink all to himself.

Bobby's father, Robert Hull, Sr., was a foreman in the cement factory. When he was younger, he had dreamed of becoming a pro hockey star. He was a good player who could skate fast and handle the puck like a wizard.

But then he got married and raised eleven children. (Bobby was the fifth.) The father transferred his dream to his eldest son.

Mr. Hull spent many long hours teaching Bobby how to play the game. Sometimes he scolded his son for sloppy stick-handling, making Bobby try again and again until he could control the puck properly.

Bobby got tired of the constant practice. But he kept it up to please his father. What the boy really enjoyed was a good, fast game of shinny. There it was every kid for himself—no passing, no teamwork, just hang onto that puck and score a goal!

By the time he was five, Bobby could play hockey much better than boys who were many years older. Mr. Hull began to believe that his son would grow up to be a star.

When Bobby was about six, in 1945, his father took him to see a pro hockey game in Toronto, 100 miles away. They saw the Maple Leafs play the Detroit Red Wings. After the game, the great Gordie Howe autographed Bobby's program. The boy never forgot the thrill.

Bobby began to play organized hockey when he was ten. When he was twelve, he played with grown men—including his father—on a team in the city of Belleville, about five miles from Point Anne.

It was there, in 1951, that he was discovered by the pros.

The Chicago Black Hawks sponsored Belleville's Junior B hockey team. The Hawks' head scout, Bob Wilson, saw Bobby on the ice one day. Later, he said: "He was the kind of boy you see once in a lifetime."

Without saying anything to the Hull family, Wilson put Bobby's name on the Chicago "negotiation" list. In effect, he reserved Bobby Hull for the Hawks whether he liked it or not.

Then Wilson told Mr. and Mrs. Hull what he had done. Mr. Hull was overjoyed. It would be Bobby's great chance! If he made good, he would not have to spend his life working in a cement plant, like his father.

Mrs. Hull was not so happy. She had dreamed that Bobby would someday go to the university. She realized that if the boy took up a hockey career, his education would suffer. Still, if the boy could become a star. . . .

The Point Anne School that Bobby attended. The waters of the Bay lie just beyond it.

Mrs. Hull finally agreed to let Bobby try for a hockey career. But it was a hard choice to make. It meant that Bobby would have to leave home at the age of 14. The Black Hawks would send him to Hespeler, Ontario for training. He would go to school there and live as a boarder with a local family.

Bobby was very lonesome in Hespeler, even though his parents tried to visit him every weekend. He stuck it out because he felt it was his duty to help the family. He worked hard practicing hockey and tried to keep up his schoolwork as well.

Bobby did very well on the Hespeler team. But Mr. Hull urged him to play better yet. Often, when the game was over Mr. Hull would say:

"You only had two goals. You should have had five."

So Bobby would try harder next time.

The Woodstock, Ontario, newspaper headlines the victory of Bobby's team.

The champion Woodstock Warriors, with Bobby third from the right in the bottom row.

The next year, Bobby was sent to the city of Woodstock, some 200 miles from home. It was the custom to switch young players around so that they would gain wide experience and receive different kinds of coaching.

The Woodstock Warriors won the Ontario Junior B championship during that 1954-55 season. And in the big victory parade, Bobby Hull rode on a fire engine wearing the chief's hat!

He was a tall, strong boy now. In the summer, he returned to Point Anne and took part-time jobs to earn money for the family. Sometimes he worked on nearby farms. He loved taking care of the animals and caring for the crops in the sunshine.

At other times, he worked in his father's cement plant. It was dusty, hot, and noisy. There were times when Bobby Hull thought:

"All the hard work of hockey will be worth it if I escape having to work *here* for the rest of my life."

The next season, Bobby was brought up to the Junior A league. Once again he lived very far from home, in St. Catharines, a large Ontario city not far from Niagara Falls.

Bobby did not play like a superstar. He was only 16, playing with older boys on Ontario's top junior team. He only scored 11 goals all season.

He had other trouble, too. Coach Rudy Pilous wanted to switch Bobby from center to left wing. The boy was a determined puck-carrier and the coach felt that a center should do more passing. But Bobby had always played center. He refused to switch and asked his parents to take him home.

Bobby sat out four games. Then both coach and player gave in. Bobby apologized to Coach Pilous, and the coach let Bobby stay on as center. But Pilous was right—and one day in the future he would prove it!

The next season, Bobby scored 33 goals, tops on the team. The fans of St. Catharines made a hero out of him. And the Black Hawk management made plans to bring Bobby to Chicago as soon as he turned 18.

Far from his family, Bobby was befriended by a lawyer named Learie who helped him through some tough days. Mr. Learie had a daughter named Judy. She and Bobby fell in love and wanted to get married.

Both sets of parents were against it. "You're too young," they said. But Bobby and Judy insisted. They married when they were 17—and were divorced a year later.

Bobby Hull played his first game against pro hockey players in 1957. The Black Hawks were training at St. Catharines and Bob Wilson invited Bobby to play with the Hawks in a practice game against the Rangers.

Bobby scored two goals.

Tommy Ivan, the manager of the Black Hawks, told Mr. and Mrs. Hull that he wanted Bobby to play his next season in the NHL. "He's ready," Ivan insisted.

If Bobby signed with the Hawks, he would not be able to graduate from high school. His parents said they would let Bobby decide.

He said: "I'll sign." And not long after, he was on his way to Chicago, a pro hockey player at last.

Tommy Ivan of the Black Hawks' management and Coach Rudy Pilous

Injuries are part of a hockey player's life. Here Bobby sports a black eye in a game against Detroit. He wore number 7 early in his career.

Bobby Hull joined the Black Hawks during the 1957-58 season. Hockey was entering a new era then. Television had discovered the game. Millions of new fans who never went to an arena were now able to watch games from their own homes. TV brought new money to the sport and new fame and publicity to the players. And the player who was destined to become the brightest hockey star of all was a husky blond boy named Bobby Hull.

His rookie year was not too sensational. He played center and still hogged the puck. He scored 13 goals the first season. But the Calder Trophy for rookie of the year went to Toronto's Frank Mahovlich, who scored 20.

Before Bobby joined the Hawks, the team had seemed to have a permanent lease on the NHL cellar. During Bobby's rookie year, they moved up a notch— to fifth.

Bobby helped. So did a new coach, who joined the team in January, 1958. He was none other than Rudy Pilous, who had coached Bobby at St. Catharines! And with the backing of Black Hawk management, he set about to rebuild the team into champions. They hadn't won a Stanley Cup since 1938. But at last things looked up.

The next season, the Hawks boasted not only Bobby Hull but also Glenn Hall, a brilliant goaltender, Pierre Pilote and Elmer Vasko on defense, and a group of rookies who would soon be the terrors of the NHL.

Young Pierre Pilote (3) scores a goal against the Maple Leafs in a 1959 game. He won the Norris trophy as outstanding defenseman in 1963, 1964, and 1965.

In 1958-59, Bobby scored 18 goals. The team made the playoffs but lost the semi-finals to the Montreal Canadiens. This magnificent team, one of the finest in hockey history, went on to win their fourth Stanley Cup in a row. They were the first team to do so.

Bobby Hull had still not hit his stride. He began to discover what was wrong that fall, when he played some exhibition games in Europe. Teamed with Eddie Shack, another man who liked to keep the puck, Bobby finally learned to lay back. He let Shack carry the puck part of the time instead of always trying to play a one-man game. Later, Bobby Hull said that this lesson—learning to pace himself—was the turning point in his career.

Star right wing Murray Balfour (8) watches the puck elude him during a game against the Bruins. At right is center Glen Slov (14). The Bruins are Fern Flaman (14) and goalie Don Simmons.

Coach Rudy Pilous forced Bobby to turn still another corner. The next season, the coach finally got his way and switched Bobby to left wing. It all worked out beautifully. Bobby won the Art Ross Trophy as league-leading scorer for the 1959-60 season.

Bobby had scored 39 goals. He and rookies Murray Balfour and Red Hay were called the "million-dollar kid" line.

The Hawks made the playoffs again. But Bobby caught a throat infection and couldn't play. Chicago bowed once more to Montreal in the semi-finals. The mighty Canadiens won their fifth Stanley Cup by taking eight playoff games in a row!

Mrs. Bobby Hull rates a smooch to build up her courage before watching Bobby play a tough game.

During that season, an ice show had come to Chicago. One of the skaters was a lovely California girl named Joanne McKay. She and Bobby were married in February, 1960.

Joanne was a level-headed young woman. In the years to come, she would help Bobby to keep his feet on the ground . . . for he was about to become a sports superstar.

Hockey itself, thanks to television, was now a major sport both in Canada and the United States. And its greatest hero was to be Bobby Hull. He was the first in his sport to receive vast publicity, the first to earn large amounts of money for endorsing products such as hockey equipment, hair tonic, and swimsuits. His income from these "sidelines" equalled his NHL salary.

Bobby signs autographs for young fans in Chicago.

He had many things going for him. He was an exciting player who drew the eyes of the crowd like a magnet. He could skate 29.2 miles per hour—fastest in the NHL. And he delighted in long dashes that brought the crowd up screaming.

He became the Golden Jet.

Bobby Hull's slap shot was legendary. It came at cringing goalies like a rifle bullet. Woe to the human flesh that was in its way! Later, a scientist clocked the speed of that shot—119.5 miles per hour.

Besides Bobby's sparkling performance, he had good looks. He was blond and handsome. Fans overlooked the scars of his trade—a constantly broken nose and missing front teeth that had fallen victims to a long-ago puck. They screamed: "Go, Bobby, go!"

And he went.

In the 1960-61 season, Bobby helped his team to a third place finish. Coach Pilous believed in tough hockey and the team racked up a record number of penalties for the season. In the semi-finals, they faced their old rivals, the Montreal Canadiens.

But this year the Canadiens were without their superb star, Maurice (Rocket) Richard. He had retired. And they were further crippled during the playoffs. Two other Montreal hockey immortals, Jean Beliveau and Bernie (Boom Boom) Geoffrion, were sidelined with injuries.

The underdog Hawks—to the surprise of all—won the semi-finals, four games to two. They went into the finals against the Detroit Red Wings. The prize would be the Stanley Cup.

In the first game of the 1961 Stanley Cup series, Bobby Hull (16) fires the third and winning goal. He went sliding over the ice after the puck. Detroit goalie Terry Sawchuk is helpless to prevent the score.

Chicago fans were wildly excited. The team had not won the Stanley Cup since 1938. And for 20 years after that, the team had been in the dumps. Only once had they made the playoffs.

But since the coming of Bobby Hull, things had looked up. Bobby was not a one-man team, however. The Hawks had other outstanding players. Pierre Pilote was a splendid defenseman who later won the Norris Trophy three years in a row. Glenn Hall later won the Vezina Trophy for goaltending. And Stan Mikita took over Bobby's old position at center. He proved to be a top scorer.

Bobby Hull (16) watches a pileup in another 1961 Stanley Cup game. Red Wing defenseman Howie Young (4) ended up on top of goalie Hank Bassen as they teamed up to prevent a score by the rushing Black Hawks. Players include Detroit's Pete Goegan (2) and Chicago's Stan Mikita (21).

A gap-toothed grin signals Bobby's joy as the Black Hawks win the Stanley Cup. The clinching game was played April 16, 1961. At right is Eric Nesterenko.

In the first game of the playoffs, Bobby scored two goals. The Black Hawks won, 3-2.

In the second game, Red Wing superstar Gordie Howe kept Bobby in check. Detroit won, 3-1. The series see-sawed back and forth. Game three went to Chicago, 3-1. Detroit took a close one in the fourth game, 2-1.

In the fifth game, the score was 1-0, Hawks, when Gordie Howie started a power play. The Detroit star and his team-mates were charging down the ice when Hawk Reggie Fleming stole the puck. Seconds later, the red light flashed. Fleming had scored and destroyed Detroit's momentum. The Hawks went on to win, 6-3. They took the next game in a walk, 5-1.

And the Stanley Cup came to Chicago for the first time in 23 years.

The next season, 1961-62, was to be Bobby's best yet. By the end of the regular season's play, he had scored 49 goals for a total of 83 points.

There remained the last game, against the New York Rangers. Their star right-winger, Andy Bathgate, was tied with Bobby for the scoring title and the Art Ross Trophy.

And still another record hung in the balance. If Bobby could score 50 goals, he would tie a record that had been reached only by Rocket Richard and Boom Boom Geoffrion.

Bobby's parents came to New York for the game. They brought a message from his kid sister, Judy. She had celebrated her birthday the day before. She said:

"Tell Robert that the only present I want is that fifieth goal!"

Mr. and Mrs. Robert Hull, Sr. check the starting lineup before a Black Hawk game.

The game was played March 25, 1962, before a sellout crowd. And not five minutes had passed before Bobby gave Judy her birthday present. Backhanding a Reg Fleming rebound, he sent the puck into the net. The crowd stood up and cheered.

Later in the game, Bathgate scored, too. But the Art Ross Trophy went to Bobby for the second time, because he had scored more goals.

As for the 51-goal record, Bobby only smiled and said: "Some season I may break it."

Bobby tries for a goal but is out-guessed by Maple Leaf goalie Johnny Bower.

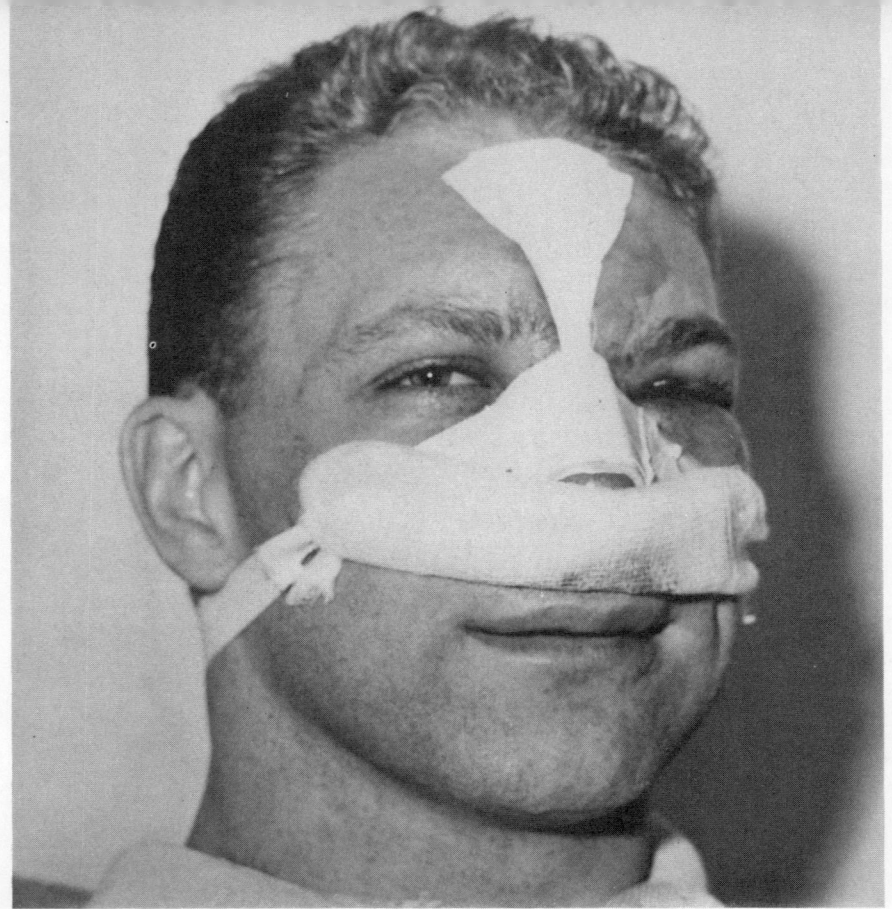

Bandages shield Bobby's smashed face.

The Black Hawks were Stanley Cup contenders again in 1962. But the favored Toronto Maple Leafs upset them, four games to two.

Bobby suffered injuries and a slump the next season. He received a badly smashed face in the semifinals, but insisted on playing in the deciding game. Doctors said he belonged in the hospital. Instead, he scored three goals and assisted on a fourth.

The effort was heroic. But it could not save the Hawks. The Red Wings won, 7-4, knocking the Hawks out of Stanley Cup contention.

In the 1962 Stanley Cup playoffs, Bobby scores a goal. The leaf players are goalie Johnny Bower and Bobby Baun. The Hawks won this game, 4-1.

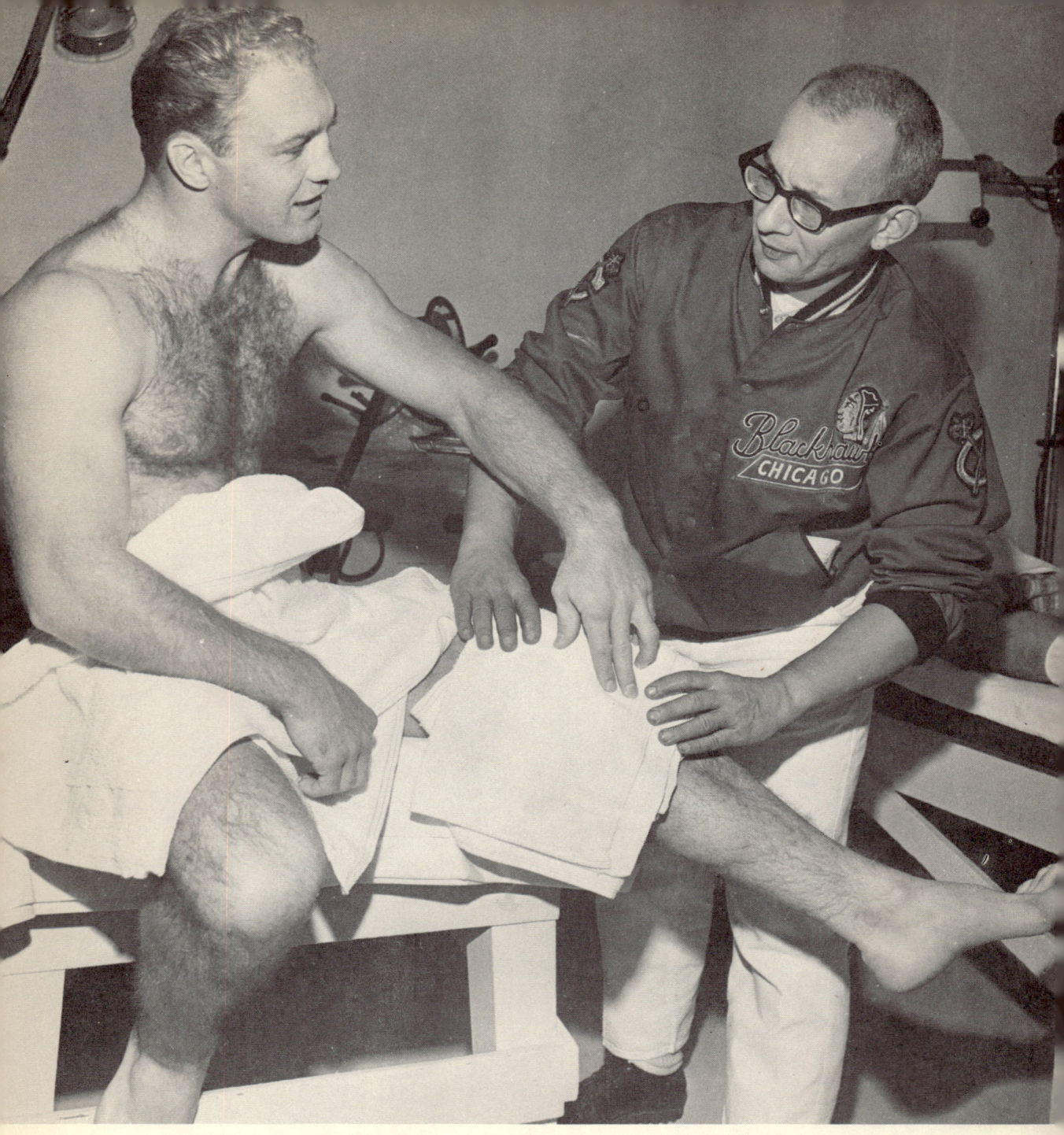

Black Hawk trainer Nick Garen applies hot packs to Bobby's injured knee. Reluctant to fight, Bobby became a target for rink rough-necks and cheap-shot artists.

Bobby Hull, Coach Billy Reay, and goalie Tony Esposito pose during a training session.

Bobby, Stan Mikita, and other Chicago players felt strongly that the coach was to blame for the team's poor showing. They pressed the owner of the Black Hawks to fire Rudy Pilous. Billy Reay became the new Chicago skipper.

The team made second place in 1963-64. But once again Detroit licked them in the semi-finals. Bobby led the league with 43 goals. It seemed only a matter of time before the 50-goal record was broken.

With each year, Bobby became a bigger favorite with the fans. Despite his many injuries, he rarely fought back. And he always took time to sign autographs and say a few words to his admirers. The more famous he became, the nicer he was. A few wise guys commented: "Can he be for real?"

He was. And the best was yet to come.

33

Bobby was always glad when the season ended. He and Joanne now had two sons, Bob and Blake. They would go home to Canada in the summer—to visit the large Hull family at Point Anne, or to live and work at a farm Bobby had bought.

Many players love hockey better than anything else. But not Bobby Hull. What he liked best was raising cattle, doing hard farm work in the sun, and being with his growing family.

Bobby raised prize Hereford cattle on his farm. He and his brother, Dennis, operated the enterprise together—with a lot of help from young Bobby, Jr. and Blake.

Bobby's brother Dennis, five years younger, worked with him on the farm. Dennis had become a fine junior hockey player for St. Catharines, just like Bobby. For the 1964-65 season, the Hawks brought Dennis up to Chicago. Both brothers were pleased. But both knew that Dennis faced a difficult future playing in the shadow of Bobby.

Dennis Hull, star left winger for the Hawks, has one of the hardest shots in hockey. He is a goaltender's terror who also shines on defense.

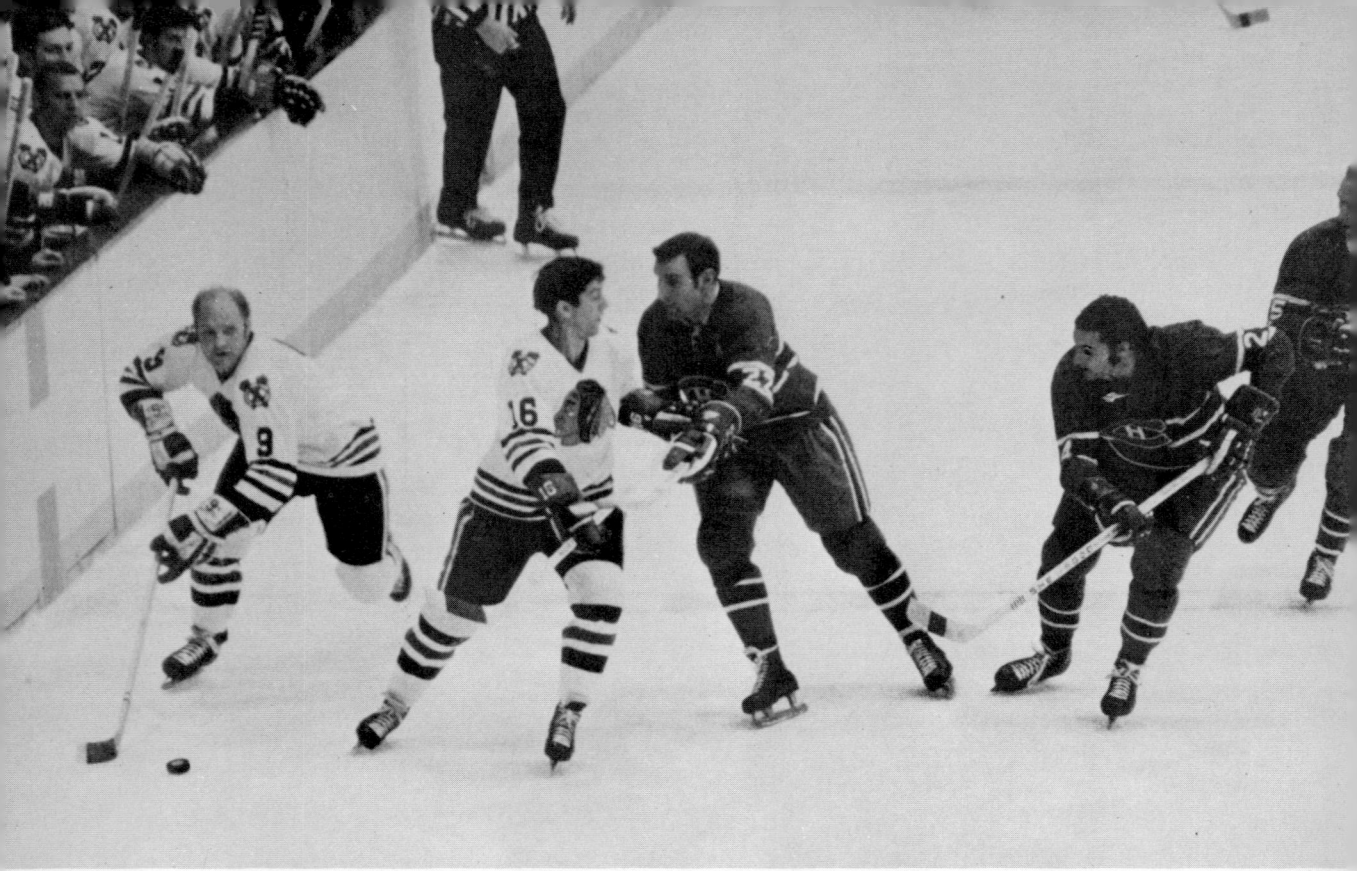

Bobby gets blocking by Chico Maki to get by John Ferguson (22) of Montreal.

Bobby Hull made a fantastic start that season. In the first 45 games, he scored 37 goals. He was greatly helped by right wing Chico Maki and by a very young center named Phil Esposito, who really knew how to feed Bobby the puck.

But luck as well as skill decides an athlete's career. When it seemed that nothing could keep him from breaking the 50-goal record, he was injured.

First one knee, then the other, was hurt. In the last 25 games of the season, he got only 2 goals. His total was only 39.

He recovered for the playoffs and helped the Hawks upset Detroit in the semi-finals. But in the finals Montreal had Claude Provost check Bobby closely. It was a tactic that would be used more and more in the years to come.

The Canadiens won the Stanley Cup by a close four games to three.

Bobby was honored with the Hart Trophy, awarded to the most valuable player. He also won the Lady Byng Trophy for sportsmanship and gentlemanly conduct. He was the first man ever to win both in a single season.

Bobby is upended by Red Wing Gary Bergman in a battle for the puck. In the background is Phil Esposito (7).

Despite his knee injury, Bobby went on another scoring spree during the 1965-66 season. He scored his 50th goal on March 22, 1966. And on March 12, Chicago Stadium was packed to overflowing with 22,000 fans, hoping to see him break the record at last.

In the third period, it was New York Rangers 2, Hawks 1. Lou Angiotti sent a pass to Bobby, who was 40 feet from the goal. His stick swung, it connected, and the puck went rocketing past goalie Cesare Maniago.

Red light! The fans erupted like a volcano. For 10 minutes they cheered and showered Bobby with hats.

But that was not the end. Bobby scored three more times to finish the season with a total of 54 goals and 97 points. He was awarded both the Hart and the Art Ross trophies.

Hockey immortals Bobby Hull and Gordie Howe got together for the All-Star game in 1970. They led the East Division to a 4-1 victory over the West. In later years, both Hull and Howe played for the WHA.

A rain of hats greets Bobby Hull's 51st goal. He became the new scoring champ of the NHL, breaking the 50-goal record shared by Rocket Richard and Boom Boom Geoffrion of Montreal.

Enough is enough—and Bobby and Phil Esposito take on Rangers' Jim Neilson (15) and Wayne Hillman (2) in a stick-swinging match in New York's Madison Square Garden.

The next season was a great one for Bobby—he scored 52 goals. It was also a Black Hawk milestone year. They finally beat "Muldoon's Curse!"

Back in 1927, the Hawks' first coach, Pete Muldoon, was fired after the first season. He is supposed to have said: "This team will never be first in the NHL."

And the Hawks never were—until 1967. Helped by Bobby, Esposito, Mikita, Red Hay and Glenn Hall, the team came out on top for the first time in history. But it was their last hurrah. They lost the semi-finals.

What was worse, the NHL was about to expand from six to twelve teams. In the process, the Chicago Black Hawks would be ruined by trades and the expansion draft.

The next year, the team finished last. This in spite of the fact that Bobby scored an incredible 58 goals.

The Hawks' great goalie, Glenn Hall, was gone to St. Louis. Young Dennis Hull was coming up fast as a top scorer. But Esposito was gone—traded to Boston, where he would become a superstar. Red Hay was gone. Bobby missed the strong centers badly. He went back to his one-man-team tactics.

Coach Billy Reay criticized Bobby for this and for skimping on back-checking and defense. The coach also said that the superstar missed too many practices because of his other businesses.

Bobby began thinking that he should retire. He would not sign a contract for the 1969-70 season until he was offered a record-breaking salary.

He was honest enough to admit his faults, however. And he improved his defensive play so vastly that the team won the division championship.

Coach Reay said: "Bobby Hull is more valuable than ever."

Dennis Hull fires a fast slap shot past New York captain Ed Westfall.

The Hawks took the Western Division title in 1970-71. Bobby saved the team in the semi-finals with two crucial goals.

For the Cup playoffs, the Hawks faced Montreal. The wily Flying Frenchmen unveiled a secret weapon, ace rookie Rejean Houle, who shadowed Bobby all over the ice. Once again, Chicago lost the championship.

Now people began to say that Bobby Orr, the young "miracle star" of the Boston Bruins, was the best player in hockey. Bobby Hull had dropped to fifth in NHL scoring. He was checked by various shadows wherever he went on the ice. It was depressing.

More than ever, he longed to retire to the farm with Joanne and their children.

Bobby Hull and his four sons pose with Olympic figure skating champion Peggy Fleming. The boys are *(left to right)* Bart, Bob, Jr., Blake, and Brett.

Bobby Hull, top hockey star of the 1960's, and Bobby Orr, top star of the 70's hold up record-breaking pucks. In a single game, played March 20, 1969, Hull scored his 54th and 55th goals, breaking his own single-season scoring record. Orr scored his 21st goal with one second left in the game, to become the highest-scoring defenseman. By coincidence, Orr celebrated his 21st birthday on the same day.

Holding a replica of the WHA "down payment" check, Bobby and his wife, Joanne express their happiness. Bobby signed with the WHA on June 27, 1972.

But a whole new career was about to open up for Bobby Hull. A new league, the World Hockey Association, was formed in 1972. Nobody took the WHA seriously until it announced that it had signed Bobby Hull.

44

Bobby wears the Jets' uniform in a practice session.

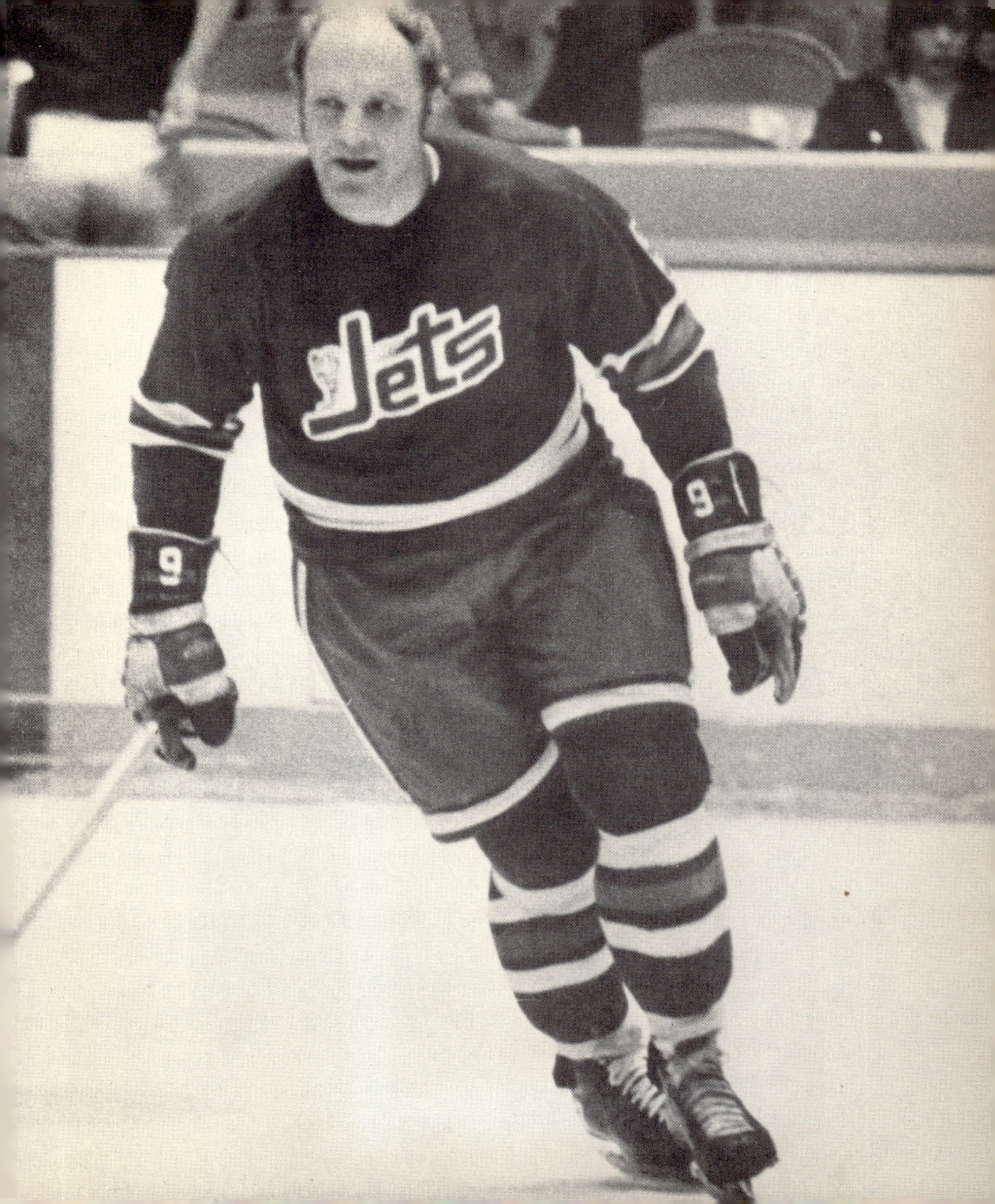
Jets

The Black Hawk management tried vainly to keep Bobby in Chicago. But his mind was made up. He went to the Winnipeg Jets—a team named after him. He would be a player-coach and also help to publicize the team and the entire WHA. For this he would be paid three million dollars over a ten-year period.

It would be a big challenge. Getting a new league going would be hard work. But Bobby believed in the WHA. He felt it would bring hockey to millions of fans who would otherwise never enjoy professional games in their own cities.

The new league had a long way to go. But it was off to a flying start on the wings of the Golden Jet.

Coaching the Jets, Bobby works hard to turn his infant team into a hockey powerhouse. In their first season, 1972-73, the Jets topped the Western Division but lost the Avco Trophy to the New England Whalers.

Bobby Hull and the Winnipeg Jets

ROBERT MARVIN HULL

He was born January 3, 1939, in Point Anne, Ontario, the fifth child and first son of Mr. and Mrs. Robert Hull, Sr. He graduated from Point Anne Grade School and attended several high schools during his amateur hockey career. Like many young players, he did not graduate. He played for Junior teams in Belleville, Hespeler, Woodstock, and St. Catharines, Ontario.

The Chicago Black Hawks brought him up to the NHL in 1957. He played 15 seasons with the Hawks before joining the WHA's Winnipeg Jets in 1972.

When Bobby was 17, he married Judy Learie. The couple had one child before they were divorced a year later. In February 1960 he married Joanne McKay. The couple has four sons and a daughter.

Bobby Hull's younger brother, Dennis, is the ninth of the Hull children. He joined the Hawks in 1964 and became an outstanding scorer. Bobby's brother Gary plays for the WHA Ottawa Nationals.

In 1967, Bobby wrote *Hockey Is My Game,* a book that tells the highlights of his earlier career and gives hockey-playing information based on his own experience.

BOBBY HULL STATISTICS

		Regular Schedule					Playoffs				
Season	Club	GP	G	A	TP	PIM	GP	G	A	TP	PIM
1957-58	Chgo.	70	13	34	47	62	—	—	—	—	—
1958-59	Chgo.	70	18	32	50	50	6	1	1	2	2
1959-60	Chgo.	70	39*	42	81*	68	3	1	0	1	2
1960-61	Chgo.	67	31	25	56	43	12	4	10	14	4
1961-62	Chgo.	70	50*	34	84*	35	12	8*	5	13	10
1962-63	Chgo.	65	31	31	62	27	5	8*	2	10	4
1963-64	Chgo.	70	43*	44	87	50	7	2	5	7	2
1964-65	Chgo.	61	39	32	71	32	14	10*	7	17*	27
1965-66	Chgo.	65	54*	43	97*	70	6	2	2	4	10
1966-67	Chgo.	66	52*	28	80	52	6	4	2	6	0
1967-68	Chgo.	71	44*	31	75	39	11	4	6	10	15
1968-69	Chgo.	74	58*	49	107	48	—	—	—	—	—
1969-70	Chgo.	61	38	29	67	8	8	3	8	11	2
1970-71	Chgo.	78	44	52	96	32	18	11	14	25	16
1971-72	Chgo.	78	50	43	93	24	8	4	4	8	6
1972-73	Winn.	63	51	52	103	37	14	9	16	25	16
1973-74	Winn.	75	53	42	95	38	4	1	1	2	4

*League leader
Ross trophy as leading scorer: 1960, 1962, 1966
Lady Byng trophy for sportsmanship: 1965
Hart trophy as most valuable player: 1965, 1966

DATE DUE

MY 17 '76	AP 05 '93	NO 11 '99	
OC 20 '76	NO 30 '93	DE 09 '99	
DE 1 '76	JA 11 '94	JA 28 '00	
OC 20 '77	OC 07 '94	FE 25 '00	
NO 28 '77	OC 25 '94	MY 08 '00	
FE 1 '78	MR 17 '95	FE 08 '01	
AP 28 '78	AP 07 '95	MR 02 '01	
JE 2 '78	AP 25 '95	NO 19 '01	
OC 30 '78	OC 09 '95	DE 20 '01	
DE 14 '79	NO 06 '95	FE 11 '02	
JA 2 '80	DE 1 '95	AP 29	
AP 1 '80	DE 10 '96		
NO 30 '90	DE 04 '97		

B May, Julian   copy 1
BOBBY HULL, HOCKEY'S GOLDEN JET
Hull

Junior High Library
Brandywine Public Schools
Niles, Michigan